Bygone Cairnbulg, Inverallochy & St Combs
with Lonmay & Crimond

by Jim Buchan

St Combs Post Office, *c.* 1908.

This book is dedicated to the memory of Jim and Sheila Buchan.
Sheila died in July 2009.
Jim died in August 2013, shortly after completing the full draft of this book.

Text © Jim Buchan, 2014.
First published in the United Kingdom, 2014,
by Stenlake Publishing Ltd.
01290 551122
www.stenlake.co.uk

ISBN 9781840336665

The publishers regret that they cannot supply copies of any pictures featured in this book.

Printed by
P2D Books, 1 Newlands Rd,
Westoning, Bedford, MK45 5LD

Acknowledgements

The family of Jim Buchan wish to acknowledge the help he received when compiling this book. Members of staff in the Reference and Local Studies Department in Aberdeen Central Library and the Special Collections team in Aberdeen University gave invaluable assistance. Our enduring thanks go to the museum services staff in Aberdeenshire Council for their help. Special thanks go to Jim's sister, Margaret Smith in Cairnbulg, for her unstinting support to Jim throughout the compilation of this book. We are grateful to Jim's Inverallochy school friends and Aberdeenshire folk for their local knowledge and expertise received over the years spent researching this book. We are also grateful for the use of additional photographs and images which appear courtesy of Billy Masson, Lorraine Noble, Joe Cardno, Hamish Stevenson, William Derby, photographer, and Crimond Kirk Session (page 35), Transporttreasury.co.uk (the photographs by W.A.C. Smith on pages 4 and; 6), Aberdeen Journals (page 11) and Aberdeenshire Council.

Mill of Crimond, *c.* 1909. This site lies to the west of Crimond.

In 1865 Philorth House was said to be a comfortable mansion with no pretensions to architectural magnificence. The oldest part of the house was probably built early in the seventeenth century for Sir Alexander Fraser, who transferred the name of the Mansion House of Philorth to his new home when he sold Cairnbulg and its castle. The house was extensively altered between 1874 and 1876 and was the seat of the Frasers of Philorth until it was destroyed by fire in 1915. The first Fraser of Philorth was the High Sheriff of Aberdeen, who distinguished himself in the Battle of Otterburn in 1388. Another of the family led horsemen supporting King Charles II at the Battle of Worcester (1651) and, rescued by his servant after being left for dead on the battlefield, went on to live until the age of 90. Another Fraser distinguished himself in the Peninsular War and at Waterloo. In 1934 Lord Saltoun purchased Cairnbulg Castle, which became the family seat again.

Philorth Halt opened on 24 April 1865 and was originally a private station for use by Lord Saltoun of Philorth House. On its opening a special circular detailed procedures for 'the station, private for Philorth House'. If Lord Saltoun or 'passengers exhibiting the written authority of Lord Saltoun' wished to board at Philorth, the distant signal showed 'Caution'. If the approaching train did not have to stop, the signal showed 'All Right'. For passengers alighting at Philorth, procedures depended on where they boarded the train. At Fraserburgh, the station master would inform 'the guard whether there were passengers or goods for Philorth. The guard [then] informed the driver.' Before starting from Lonmay or Rathen, guards on down trains ascertained whether there were passengers or goods for Philorth and then instructed the driver. The halt was later in general use but closed to goods on 26 July 1926 (at which time it also became unstaffed). It closed completely on 4 October 1965 and is now a dwelling.

On a knoll near the Water of Philorth, two miles from Fraserburgh and less than a mile from the North Sea, the Manor House of Philorth was part of the coastal defence planned by the Comyn Earls of Buchan. In the War of Independence in the late thirteenth century, the Comyns supported the English and after Robert the Bruce defeated them in 1308, the king destroyed the 'Comyn castles' and gave Comyn lands to his supporters. The estate of Cairnbulg passed to the Earl of Ross's family and when his daughter married Sir Alexander Fraser her dowry was the Ross land in Buchan: the Frasers of Philorth had arrived! They restored the manor house, later converted to the Z-plan Cairnbulg Castle. Over the centuries it was sold several times until, severely storm-damaged, it was derelict when purchased for the Duthie family of shipbuilders in Aberdeen. It was restored for John Duthie in 1896/97 with instructions that the exterior be made 'as near as might be, a reproduction of the castle, as it was three centuries ago'. The towers were repaired and linked by a frontage 66 feet in length. Internally, the kitchen, scullery, larder, pantries and servants' hall and bedrooms were on the ground floor while dining and drawing rooms were on the first floor and furnished with pitch pine and dark oak. Seven bedrooms were 'models of ingenuity and taste'. An oil-driven dynamo supplied lighting by electricity, 'a mode hitherto unknown in the locality'. Gas lighting was also provided and spring water was pumped up by windmill. The restoration cost over £5,000 and the 'beautifying of the surroundings another four figures'. The castle is now open to the public by appointment only.

Provided primarily for residents of Cairnbulg Castle, Philorth Bridge Halt was on the St Combs Light Railway which opened on 1 July 1903. After a debate in 1932 about a site for a cemetery for Inverallochy and Cairnbulg, it was established at Mains Brae on Cairnbulg estate. One Inverallochy resident was so incensed that he declaimed, in Doric, 'You can all do as you wish but I'll never be buried in it as long as I live!' A former Cairnbulg station master recalled that the London and North Eastern Railway ran 'funeral trains for a year or two' from the village to the halt, which was near the new cemetery. The halt closed to goods services on 7 November 1960 and to passengers on 3 May 1965.

The Shore, Cairnbulg. *Pollable Persons Aberdeen 1696* is a unique source of information on the origins of some of the villages in this area. Printed from a manuscript discovered in the library of Gordon of Cairness, the two volumes record the collection of a poll tax and give names, locations, and occupations of all the inhabitants of Aberdeenshire in 1696, 'excepting children under sixteen years and beggars'. For Cairnbulg it names '5 whytefishers, tenants of Lord Fraser' and '12 Whitefishers belonging to Cairnbulg', tenants of Patrick Ogilvie. In her 'Papers', a document of recollections of the area written between the late nineteenth century and the 1920s, Christian Watt tells how, walking on the beach from Fraserburgh to Cairnbulg, she 'came first to Brandesburgh, founded by Patrick Ogilvie', who 'coaxed some folk from Cairnbulg to start a new tounie in order to cut in on the sea's bounty.' The 1861 census lists 87 houses in Cairnbulg with 427 residents; 36 were fisherwomen while of the 113 male workers, 105 were fishermen. Not named in *Pollable Persons* or the 1861 census, Brandesburgh was at the northwestern end of Cairnbulg. Its landing shore is now part of Cairnbulg Boat Haven, a marina, which is also used by small fishing boats. Lord Fraser's 'whytefishers' used the shore in the foreground of this photograph from around 1915; the distant boats are in Inverallochy.

In 1786 the Act for Erecting Certain Lighthouses in the Northern Parts of Great Britain established the Northern Lighthouse Board (NLB), responsible for erecting lighthouses in Scotland, and the following year the first NLB lighthouse was established in an old castle on Kinnaird Head. In 1858 the NLB erected a beacon at Cairnbulg Point, but this was merely a standard known as a marker beacon or day mark beacon that was painted red and not fitted with a light, and thus not fit for purpose after dark. Recalling 'the vessels, including steam trawlers, which had come to grief there in the previous quarter of a century', Fraserburgh Harbour Board later lobbied the Northern Lighthouse Commissioners, claiming that 'Fraserburgh Bay, from Kinnaird Head to Cairnbulg Point, a stretch of fully two miles, was lacking in lighting for mariners passing the dangerous reef known as The Briggs at Cairnbulg.' As a result the commissioners fitted a light, costing £605, to the original standard. Operational from June 1914, and flashing twice every ten seconds, this beacon had local men as keepers (attendants) – J. Summers until 1942, R. Duthie until 1961, and then A. Buchan. The light used acetylene from 1914, dissolved acetylene from 1946, and solar panels from 1993. It still stands although it now has a safety frame and railings around the light.

Opened on the St Combs Light Railway on 1 July 1903 and originally named Inverallochy, this station was renamed Cairnbulg on 1 September the same year after demands from residents. Beyond the fence on the left, a loading/unloading area with track for trucks served the needs of residents and played a vital role in the Second World War as it was delivery point for construction materials for the building of an airfield nearby. The station had a rounding loop: if the train was not going to St Combs, the engine moved on the loop to the other end of the train for the return journey to Fraserburgh. The Light Railway Order limited the weight of engines and rolling stock and set a maximum speed of 25 mph; after using the rounding loop, an engine travelling tender foremost was limited to 15 mph. The house on the extreme right of the photograph was the Inverallochy Kirk manse. The station closed in 1965.

On 18 April 1905 the platform at Cairnbulg Station was crowded with passengers going to Maud to persuade the Licensing Court to withhold an alcohol licence from the new Cairnbulg Station Hotel. The solicitor for the applicant said, 'the light railway brought a large number of businessmen to the villages and many golfers came to play on the course.' He stressed the lack of accommodation locally, where 'refreshment, either for man or beast, could not be got.' His opponent argued that, with no gates on the level crossing, 'anyone coming out of the hotel in a drunken state might come by a serious accident.' The application was refused. Two local men bought the hotel building and shared family apartments in it. After changing hands several times, it became a private house in 2003.

The *New Statistical Account of Scotland* of the 1840s says Cairnbulg and Inverallochy are 'very contiguous fishing villages'. The traditional boundary marker between the villages, a small stream called the Strype, now flows to the coast in an underground pipe, but where the road into the villages forks the modern road signs show that – separated only by the width of the road to Cairnbulg on the left – they are still 'very contiguous'. This photograph appeared in the *Press and Journal* of 13 March 1976 with the caption, 'Mr John Buchan gives tuition to the up and coming flute band recruits of Inverallochy and Cairnbulg. Left to right, back row: Graham Tait, Alan Buchan, Ian Anderson, Kevin West and John Cardno; front row: Albert Ritchie, Brian Ritchie, Michael Tait, Adam Tait and Gordon West.' Flute (fife) bands play in the villages' annual Temperance Walks.

Inverallochy shore. *Pollable Persons Aberdeen* 1696 lists '19 Whyte fishers belonging to Inverallochy' but it is not known when the village was founded. Looking northward from Inverallochy, this view shows the houses along the Cairnbulg foreshore. The Strype – the small stream marking the boundary between the 'twin villages' – flows into the sea, in an underground pipe, beyond the boats beached on the right above the high water level on the Inverallochy shore. These yawls, oar and sail driven, were in regular use for inshore fishing. The others on the left were beached temporarily on the landward side of the shore while – in larger boats that were berthed at Fraserburgh when not in use – their crews were engaged elsewhere in a seasonal fishery, e.g. the Minch or Yarmouth. Some families moved to Fraserburgh for the summer herring fishing, returning to the villages between seasons to fish in the yawls, using handlines and smalins. Made of lighter cord than the great-lines used in the big boats in the white fish season in the Minch, a smalin (small-line) was about 50 fathoms long (300 feet) and had around 100 barbed hooks tied to it at regular intervals. Baited with mussels, limpets, sand eels or lugworms, smalins were set on white fish grounds and left overnight to be hauled next day.

According to etymologists Gowanhole is not associated with the flower, Gowan (daisy), but indicates that before inshore fishermen in the southern end of Inverallochy required houses and a landing shore there was a cattle-fold opposite the gap in the rocks. The upturned yawls near the houses on the foreshore suggest that their crews were engaged in one of the seasonal fisheries aboard their bigger vessels. Houses along the shoreline were built with a gable to the sea to minimise the adverse effects of North Sea storms. The 1861 census of Inverallochy records 128 houses with 652 residents, of whom 59 were fisherwomen and, of 152 male workers, 139 were fishermen.

In April 1843 the *Aberdeen Journal* reported, 'the congregation in the New Church at Inverallochy presented a Pulpit Gown and several books to the Rev. Alexander Cobban, the missionary appointed by the Presbytery.' Charles Ogg, appointed 'preacher in the local mission station' in 1848, became minister of the *quoad sacra* parish of Inverallochy when it was disjoined from Rathen in 1864. Ordained in 1881, the Rev. Duncan Macgregor – Gaelic scholar fluent in Hebrew and Greek – became a legend when typhoid was rife in the villages. He 'ministered' to the sick until he was infected himself. Recovered, he served as parish minister until he died in 1923. The unguarded railway crossing, on the only road into the 'twin villages', is shown here; notices were posted to warn traffic to 'Beware of the Trains'. The school building is to the right of the church.

Inverallochy's original war memorial was this 'miniature clock tower' which was dedicated on Sunday, 30 May 1920. There had been some debate as to whether the village hall should be enlarged to become a memorial hall, but this design won out. By the late 1940s, however, it was considered 'out of date' and a memorial committee was established to collect money for a new design. It took four years to raise the required £800 and on Sunday, 14 December 1952 the present memorial was unveiled and dedicated on the same site as its predecessor (the site is within the grounds of Inverallochy school).

Inverallochy Golf Club was founded in 1888. On 26 August 1902, the eighteen-hole course at Whitelinks, between Inverallochy and Charleston, was described in the *Fraserburgh Herald*. The longest hole measured 450 yards and the others between 190 and 300 yards. The Long Hole had a deep hazard 100 yards from the tee, and bents on the further side. The Allochy Burn was a hazard on the seventh. The fifteenth, 'Perplexity' on the score card, with its green on a plateau ringed by bents, was a 'very sporting hole'. The deeply rutted seventeenth needed 'careful negotiation' and 'Sodom, AKA Charleston' had to be played to 'have its characteristics understood'. With the club captain – dominie (schoolmaster) David Dundas, known as Dasky – holding the pin on the sixteenth green in this photograph, members were learning the 'characteristics' of the course. They never lost a match against a visiting club!

In April 1904 East Aberdeenshire's MP, Mr Maconochie, arranged for twelve Inverallochy Golf Club members to play crack Scottish amateurs at Barnton and Musselburgh. Photographed with their hosts in Edinburgh, after losing both matches, their defeat was attributed to their being unaccustomed to the ultra smooth surfaces of the greens and the 'gutty' (gutta-percha) balls they used. The opposition's Haskell balls, known as 'bouncing billies', outdistanced gutties by up to 25 yards a stroke. The Inverallochy players used Haskells thereafter! On 26 April the *Fraserburgh Herald*, reporting the Edinburgh matches, quoted a London periodical's suggestion, 'Could the Royal St George's at Sandwich or the Deal and Littlestone clubs not arrange a match with the Inverallochy men ere they go down in the boats to the sea next month?'

Mr Maconochie, at his own expense, arranged a match for Saturday, 1 April 1905 at Royal St George's, between ten Inverallochy club golfers and MPs, including the Prime Minister. The ten members of the team travelled overnight, arriving on Thursday, 30 March at King's Cross. After breakfast, they were shown the 'sights' – the Mansion House, the Royal Exchange, the Tower, St Paul's (voted most impressive), the National Gallery and Buckingham Palace. They had a tour of the Houses of Parliament, enjoyed a smoke on the terrace, and then sat in the Strangers' Gallery. They took it all in their stride and, in the evening, were guests of honour in the front row of the Empire Theatre. On Friday, they went to Sandwich to practise for next day's match.

Taken during match play at Sandwich, this photograph is shown courtesy of Joe Cardno, whose grandfather, James Whyte, is featured with team captain, William Whyte, and opponents J. L. Walkyn and, author, explorer, and big game hunter, Sir Henry Seton-Karr. On 29 May 1914 – sailing home in the *Empress of Ireland* after a hunting trip in British Columbia – he was among the 1,012 who drowned when the boat sank in the St Lawrence after colliding with the Norwegian freighter *Storstad*. Reporting the disaster, the *Fraserburgh Herald* said that William Whyte had a club, signed nine years previously by the former MP, and 'During the past few days, numerous members of the golfing fraternity have called to see the club.'

'Expert' advice to the Inverallochy club stressed that a professional would be advantageous to the 'rising generation'. A journalist wrote, 'A mania for golf pervades in the village. There is a junior club of schoolboys, who could give many an average team a close tussle for victory. Dundas is both golfer and dominie and every encouragement is given to boys to learn the game. Urchins may be seen, at all times in the street, swinging away at corks with all kinds of clubs.' One urchin, William Ritchie, born 1894, seen here swinging away at a cork on Mid Street, Inverallochy, became one of the best local golfers. After being surfaced, the street was nicknamed the New Road. Replicating the 'gable to the sea' alignment on the shoreline, the houses are also 'gable to the street'.

In 1877 the Royal National Lifeboat Institution (RNLI) decided to establish a lifeboat station at Whitelinks Bay between Inverallochy and Charleston. Local residents undertook to share the cost of 'a substantial and commodious boathouse' and to give, collectively, around £30 annually to help to meet recurrent expenses. The laird gifted a site for a granite-built boathouse and the first lifeboat arrived by rail on 2 March 1878, at Rathen where it was off-loaded to a carriage and a ceremonial welcome. When it reached Inverallochy, Mrs Gordon of Cairness named the boat 'Robert Adamson' (Miss Eliza Adamson of Dundee had given £329 for a lifeboat to be named in memory of her brother who had died in 1873.) This photograph was taken on the occasion of a 'Free Gift Sale' in aid of the RNLI, held by the Fraserburgh lifeboat crew and their wives on 26 April 1933 in the town's Dalrymple Hall. Shipbuilders lent an old horse-drawn lifeboat carriage to the crew, who painted a sailing boat to resemble an old lifeboat. The boat, carrying a banner advertising the sale, was pulled through the town by horses, preceded by flautists from Cairnbulg and Inverallochy.

After they helped to publicise the 'Free Gift Sale' by leading the horse-drawn 'old lifeboat' along the principal streets of Fraserburgh, members of flute bands from Cairnbulg and Inverallochy posed on the metal stairway outside the Dalrymple Hall. On the day, members of bands from the villages played in harmony with each other, reflecting the high esteem in which they held the lifeboat men. Usually they vied with each other to be biggest and/or best, when they, singly, were leading Temperance walks in the villages – Inverallochy on Christmas Day, Cairnbulg on New Year's Day, and St Combs on Aal Eel (Auld Yule), Old Christmas Day, 6 January. Currently, Inverallochy and Cairnbulg walks are held on the dates as stated. To suit holidays, St Combs Walk is held on 2 January.

Inverallochy Castle, four miles from Fraserburgh and nearer to St Combs than Inverallochy, was not 'built for coastal defence'. John B. Pratt says, 'the castle belonged to the Comyns and was probably built by one of that family. There is no date to the building, and no satisfactory account can be obtained of its origin and fortunes.' The *Statistical Account of Scotland* confirms that at the end of the eighteenth century, a stone formerly placed over the entrance was found in the vicinity. The stone has vanished but different versions of a rhyming inscription, linking the castle with the Abbey of Deer, have survived. Macgibbon and Ross say 'the rhyme gives no information as to the date of the castle'. They thought Sir William Comyn of Inverallochy, Lyon King-of-Arms in 1514, built it around that time.

An anonymous donor paid £441 for a lifeboat built by D. & W. Henderson & Co. in the Meadowside Yard on the Clyde. Named 'Three Brothers', it arrived at Rathen lifeboat station at Whitelinks Bay on 27 May 1889 to replace the 'Robert Adamson'. Most of the local fishermen were working 'away from home' and so the boat did not receive the planned welcome of its predecessor. Self-rightable when capsized, and driven by ten oars and two sails as appropriate, it is seen here with 'Tipping's Wheel Plates'. Mounted on the carriage's big wheels to prevent them sinking into the sand, the plates were inadequate sometimes and horses had to pull the boat to the water. In a synchronised operation, the crew began to row when men on the beach pulled on traces to launch the boat from its carriage. Before the station was closed in 1905, in thirteen launches fifteen lives were saved.

The last edition of the *Aberdeen Journal* from 1801 and the first six editions of 1802 announced, 'Mrs MACKENZIE, Proprietor of INVERALLOCHY, having resolved to erect another Seatown on that part of her property called Mill of Links, Fishermen desirous to settle there, will know particulars on applying to Baillie Kelman, Fraserburgh, factor on the estate. In regard to the situation, it is well known to be one of the most pleasant on the coast, and the landing place safe, and of easy access.' Thus, Charleston, Rathen, was founded, with a wooden bridge and a ford across the Mill Burn from St Combs. By 1861 Charleston had fourteen houses and 73 residents, including 53 surnamed Buchan! There were eight fisherwomen and a tailor who was the only one of 22 male workers not a fisherman. St Combs residents, known locally as 'New Tooners', revealed their opinion of their neighbours in Charleston by branding it Sodom.

The shore at St Combs. *Pollable Persons Aberdeen 1696* lists eleven fisher families in Lonmay and the *Statistical Account of Scotland* of 1793–95 says a fishing-town in Lonmay, was 'lately built of 20 tiled houses, placed in two parallel rows, with a street in the middle.' The *Third Statistical Account* of 1951 identifies the fishing-town as St Combs, 'founded in 1771 by the laird of Cairness, who gave £5 Scots to each of 20 fishermen to build on the new site and operate from there.' The houses – 18 feet, 9 inches by 12 feet, 3 inches, with 5 feet to the eaves and 9 feet, 5 inches to the ridge – were earthen floored, whinstone-built, with two small windows but no chimneys. In 1861 St Combs had 99 houses and 460 residents, including 68 fisherwomen and, of 125 male workers, 120 fishermen.

KIRKLAKES, ST. COMBS

This landing shore is near a cemetery, about 150 yards from the sea, at the site of St Colm's Kirk. In his book *Buchan*, John B. Pratt speaks of 'The fishing village of St Combs (a corruption of St Colm's)', i.e. he links the name of the village with St Colm, an evangelist here before Columba came from Ireland to Iona. Etymologists interpret 'lakes', from the Celtic *Leacan*, as 'smooth, flat rocks polished by the passage of an ice-sheet in the glacial period'. The small portable rollers on which the yawls were pulled above the high water level and launched when required are visible on the left, under the keel of FR 407. Like other village boats, this was registered in Fraserburgh.

Behind the old schoolhouse in St Combs, near a path leading to the shore, members of smalin-fisher families are seen here 'pairtin' (sharing) a bulk delivery of mussels. Once shared, the mussels were sown on scaups (scattered in areas suitable for mussel beds), where they became attached to rocks and were kept alive by the ebb and flow of the tide until required. The eight men pictured – all Buchans or Bruces – reflect the preponderance in the fishing villages of a limited number of surnames. This led to a culture of nicknames ('tee-names' or 'by-names') to assist identification. Here, they were Gib's Willie, Hock's Sandy, Auld Hunnert, Little Willie, Jockie Bo, Bielder's Jock, Pow's Geordie and Pow. Mrs Strachan was known as Megsie!

Overleaf: St Combs had no piped water supply until 1933. Previously, water for drinking and cooking had to be carried from the Brick Well, near the shore beyond the old schoolhouse. Some enterprising young teenagers became water carriers to earn a few pence but, in the division of labour within a fisher family, the water carrier was often a woman with a yoke across her shoulders and two pails, whence the phrase 'a fracht of water' entered the local dialect. ('Fracht' – what can be carried at one time.) Local lore relates that although piped water was available, several residents said the newly laid pipes were dirty and continued to use water from the well!

The 'trunks' (creels) on the right of this photograph were used to catch lobsters and crabs. In 1925, with thirteen boats engaged, St Combs's 'trunk season' peaked before the summer herring season. The catch, averaging ten and a half hundredweights per week per boat, was sent by rail to Billingsgate Market, London. Cod nets were used to catch small species of white fish. Attached to a hook driven into a wall, the net on the ground is being mended by the woman standing beside it. The woman next to the wall was a typical fisherman's wife with hair in a bun and knitting needles in her hands, and she dressed the men in her family with homemade items such as a 'linner' (winter vest), made from a length of flannel and like a sack with holes for arms and head, thigh-length stockings for long, leather sea-boots, and drawers (underpants) and (ganseys) jerseys which were knitted with thick wool. Socks and items for 'go-ashores' (leisure dress) were made of thinner wool.

This postcard of St Combs was produced by Peter Buchan who ran the local post office. As well as doing the household chores and helping with preparations for inshore fishing, many village women became fisherwomen or fishwives and walked miles to sell or barter their fish for farm produce. The fish was dried or smoked to extend its 'sell-by' dates.

CENTRAL VIEW, ST. COMBS

The Light Railway Act of 1896 was designed to encourage the building of less expensive railways. In 1899 a Light Railway Order approved a line from Fraserburgh to St Combs via Kirkton Bridge Halt, Philorth Bridge Halt and Cairnbulg Station. When the line was opened on 1 July 1903 the *Aberdeen Daily Journal* said 'difficulties necessitated delay [but] once they were overcome, construction was completed and the first service of trains inaugurated within a period of ten months.' Local lore says village residents donated money, or worked on the project, to ensure its completion. Unfenced fields meant engines were fitted with cowcatchers on the front and the rear. The *People's Journal* reported that the St Combs line carried 50,000 passengers in its first six months.

The area just behind the station, with West Street running up through the centre of the photograph and the school (long since replaced by more substantial buildings) on the right. The station closed on 3 May 1965.

Rattrayhead, Rattray. *Pollable Persons Aberdeen 1696* lists ten fishers in Crimond – four in the burgh of Rattray, three at Mains of Haddo, two at Broadland, and one at Bilbo. There was no fish town in the parish in 1792, but 'some of the crofters and artificers, on the estates of Broadland and Haddo, fish in good weather, when they are not otherwise employed. Mr Harvey of Broadland proposes to make a proper landing place, but has not yet begun to put his plan in execution.' He 'wanted immediately several steady fishermen' when he advertised Rattrayhead fish town in June 1795. In July 1838 it was 'for let with a right to take mussels from the rocks'; five fishermen were recorded in the 1861 census. Nicknamed 'Botany' (shades of the Australian convict settlement), and with the continuing menace of the Rattray Briggs (see next page) and no easily accessible, safe landing place, Rattrayhead did not flourish as a fish town.

From 1871 to 1883, 24 vessels were wrecked on Rattray Briggs, a reef lying at right angles to the coast. The Northern Lighthouse Board engaged David A. Stevenson to erect Rattray Head Lighthouse a quarter of a mile offshore on the Briggs, with its foundation on the Ron Rock above the surface at low water but beneath it at high water. Due to this and problems with delivering raw materials, the work took about three years. The base, solid to a height of eighteen feet, was built with 4,000 tons of concrete and 20,000 cubic feet of granite blocks, each weighing from one and a half to two tons. Over 100,000 white enamelled fire-clay bricks and a granite coping were used for the tower, topped by a copper-roofed dome holding a parabolic lens and Argund lamps fuelled by whale oil. These used hollow wicks, with a current of air passing through, which gave a clean non-smoky flame. Operational from 1895 and flashing three times every 30 seconds, the light was visible up to fifteen miles away. When an automated light was installed in 1981/82, the old lens was moved to Aberdeen Maritime Museum. It remains on display, showing the damage done by a Luftwaffe machine gunner during a hit-and-run raid in mid summer 1944 when the bombs dropped failed to explode.

The coastguard houses at Rattrayhead, *c.* 1915. These still stand but are derelict. The coastguard lookout post is in the background. Coastal changes led to the formation in the early eighteenth century of the Loch of Strathbeg, formerly a lagoon leading to open sea, and to the closure of a small harbour near the Castle Hill of Rattray at Starnakeppie which had been frequented by Dutch fishing vessels. The final stage of this transformation came in a storm in 1720 which engulfed the harbour with shifting sands so suddenly that a vessel was trapped and cut off from the sea. The loss of the harbour led to the decline of the Royal Burgh of Rattray, which had been founded by Queen Mary in 1564 to end disputes over the superiority of the existing village between the Earl of Erroll and the Earl Marischal.

Tradition says that early in the thirteenth century a son of a Comyn Earl of Buchan drowned in a well at Rattray, where St Mary's Chapel 'was founded for his soul'. The *New Statistical Account* refers to this chapel when it describes 'walls of a chapel (surrounded by a burying-ground), still in excellent preservation. The length within the walls is 45 feet, the breadth 18 feet, the thickness of the walls 3 feet, and the height of the gables 32 feet. The walls are built of very small stones firmly cemented together with lime. Around this chapel formerly stood the burgh of Rattray.' With a weekly market and twice yearly fair, Rattray did not prosper, especially after the loss of the 'harbour' at Starnakeppie (see page 32). In its latter years the market was held near Dipplebrae Farm, at a former staging post between Peterhead and Fraserburgh, but was discontinued in the early 1860s.

The 23rd Psalm to the tune 'Crimond' is included in the revised hymnal for the Church of Scotland (2005), credited as 'Possibly by Jessie Seymour Irvine (1836–1887) or David Grant (1833–1893)'. This ignores the *Third Statistical Account of Scotland* (1953) in which the Rev. W. D. Russell says 'Crimond' was harmonised by David Grant, at the request of Miss Jessie Seymour Irvine, known locally as 'Seymour', who composed the tune in the manse at Crimond, seen here, when her father was the parish minister. In *The Kirks of Buchan Presbytery*, a publication to mark the year 2000, Mrs Patricia Russell, widow of the Rev. W. D. Russell, says Seymour composed 'Crimond' as an exercise when attending a class for organists. She asked David Grant to harmonise it and, 'Consequently he was credited with having composed it.'

Part of a wall remains of the first known Crimond Church, built in 1576. Erected in 1812 and refurbished in 1895, the present church is about half a mile from the ruin. The clock, made in London in 1817, was used at Haddo (Crimond) Farm until James Laing gave it to the church. Showing the text 'The hour's coming', it is famous for its hour of 61 minutes! In 1949 a minute, between XI and XII, was removed but this caused such a furore in the village that it was restored. In 1994 an electric clock was installed and the original movement put on display in the church in memory of the late Councillor Norman Cowie OBE, who, with 58 years, set a record as longest-serving local councillor in Scotland. A special service was held to dedicate the new clock, complete with text and 61 minutes.

Planned by Aberdeen architect, Archibald Simpson, Crimonmogate House cost over £10,000 when built for Sir Charles Bannerman in 1825. Forty years later the house, 'within easy distance of Lonmay Station', was featured in a description of the Formartine and Buchan Railway: 'Built of granite in the classic style of architecture, and of pleasing though not gigantic proportions, it has a fine porch of the Grecian order.' The estate was 'every year presenting a more improved aspect. Within the last twenty or thirty years, a large extent of wasteland has been reclaimed within the bounds. This includes more than a hundred acres of moss and moor. Many new farm steadings, too, have recently sprung up. A good deal has been done in planting beltings (small areas of woodland) on different parts of the property with the view of affording increased shelter, and, at the same time, of beautifying the place.' Later, Charles McKean describes an 'elegant and commodious mansion . . . [It] has a weighty, Doric-columned and pedimented portico protruding between projecting wings [but] its purity was sadly compromised by a lumpish mansard roof with round-headed dormer windows added c. 1860.' During the Second World War the house was commandeered for the Consolidated Pneumatic Tool Company office staff from London.

Inheritances, including sugar plantations, made Charles Gordon of Buthlaw the richest man in Buchan. In 1782 his estate mansion house was built at Cairness, Lonmay, but he then decided to erect a grander mansion and engaged James Playfair as architect. Work began in 1791 and although Playfair died in 1793, his plans were used and the house, costing about £25,000, was finished in 1799. The *New Statistical Account* refers to 'the principal mansion in Lonmay, the House of Cairness', with 'a porch, which is a very chaste construction after the Grecian model, having four Ionic pillars, of granite'. Charles Gordon's son, Thomas, an officer in the Royal Greek Army, led the relief of Athens in 1827 and wrote *The History of the Greek Revolution*. He built a smaller replica of Cairness House at Argos, Greece, but returned to Cairness, where he died in 1841.

Playfair's remit was to absorb the existing house in a grander mansion. His solution, which included the new frontage seen in the previous photograph, contained eight reception rooms, seventeen bedrooms, five bathrooms, two staff flats, and the 'court of offices' seen here. The granite used in specified places came from Cairngall Quarry, Longside, but the body of the house is 'built of stone the masons call heathen, quarried on the estate'. It was given 52 Doric column metal chimney cans, shipped from London via Peterhead, and friezes of Egyptian hieroglyphics. Cairness was judged 'one of the most important neoclassical houses in the UK'. Some of the head office staff of the Consolidated Pneumatic Tool Company (CPT), evacuated from London during the Second World War, lived and worked there (their colleagues occupied Crimonmogate House). Fraserburgh's three CPT factories worked 24 hours daily making pneumatic tools, parts of Bofors anti-aircraft guns, and boosters for Rolls Royce aero engines for Spitfires and Hurricanes.

Cairness Lodges, Lonmay.

Using Playfair's plans, the lodges and associated metalwork – seen here – were built in 1891. The A-listed house had a chequered history after the Second World War. An English architect-cum-architectural historian and his interior designer wife bought it from a local farmer and held musical evenings for paying guests to help to finance restoration work. Their target, 'a concert, with 30 guests in the drawing room, each sitting on a chair of the same period as the house', proved too ambitious. New owners, a Lebanese journalist and a Spanish artist, who studied Contemporary Art History at Sotheby's Institute in London, continued the work of restoration while catering for bed and breakfast guests, but the house was put on the market in 2013 for £2,000,000.

The parish church at Lonmay. Pratt's *Buchan* says 'Till 1607, the Parish Church, dedicated to St Columba, the saint of the parish, was situated near the seashore, in the village of St Colm's. In 1607, [it] was removed from St Colm's to the more central situation it now occupies.' A new parish church, seen here, was built southwest of St Combs, about a quarter of a mile from its predecessor, and dedicated in 1788. Charles McKean describes it as 'A rather attractive T-plan Georgian box-kirk with large square windows, the usual birdcage bellcote on the west gable, and an interior of particular interest: the galleries are supported on twin columns, and there survives the original pulpit and fine sounding board.' It is still in use today.

Lonmay Post Office. James Forrest was listed as postmaster here in a trade directory from 1878. Letters arrived from Fraserburgh and the north and Aberdeen and the south twice a day; despatches were also made in both directions twice a day. Other facilities included a money order and telegraph office and a savings bank.

Bank House and the local petrol station, Lonmay.

The Formartine and Buchan Railway was approved in 1858, with a junction at Mintlaw for lines to Peterhead and Fraserburgh. Dyce was linked to Peterhead in 1862 but financial and engineering problems led to a successful bid the following year for an Act of Parliament to modify the plan for the line to Fraserburgh. With a junction at Maud instead of Mintlaw, the line – via stations at Brucklay, Strichen, Mormond Halt, Lonmay, Rathen, and Philorth ('the station private for Philorth House') – was opened in 1865 and in 1866 all Aberdeenshire lines were amalgamated within the Great North of Scotland Railway (GNSR). On the Knowsie estate, Lonmay Station was only four and a half miles by road from St Combs. Fishwives paid reduced fares and were allowed one creel of fish, free of charge, on GNSR trains and so Lonmay Station became a starting point for their canvassing of the area southward to Maud Junction.

A snowstorm blanketed Aberdeenshire on the Sunday and Monday of 27/28 December 1908. The *Aberdeen Daily Journal* reckoned it 'constituted a 'record' for continuousness' and reported 'roads are blocked and quite impassable, while drifting has been general'. On 30 December reports from the districts showed that the storm had increased in violence and traffic of all kinds had been stopped. This scene at Lonmay Station was replicated at other stations on the line. On Hogmanay, plate glass windows were blown in by a windstorm in Fraserburgh, where wreaths (deep drifts) were fifteen feet deep. On 4 January 1909 the *Journal*'s readers would have been pleased to learn that 'after about a week's isolation, railway communication with Peterhead and Fraserburgh was re-established on Saturday. The work of clearing the lines occupied nearly four days.'

Mormond House was originally named Cortes House and was built early in the nineteenth century on Cortes estate for John Gordon of Cairnbulg. Cortes, derived from Gaelic for circle, recalls a prehistoric stone circle on the estate. When the estate was sold in 1867, Mormond House was described as having 'an elegant portico over the main entrance, gas and water from private sources, and a garden with vinery, greenhouse, and propagating house'. Within a mile of Lonmay Station, five miles of Fraserburgh harbour and twelve of Peterhead harbour, the house had 'communication with all parts of the Kingdom'. Of the estate's 1,600 acres, 1,000 were arable and over 400 moor or 'improvable pasture'. With a water-driven sawmill and a threshing mill, the home farm was the first in Buchan to reap with scythes, introduced by John Gordon after seeing them used in England.

These houses stand on what is now the A90. The shop property and adjacent house are now a single dwelling known as Rose Cottage.

The peaks of Mormond Hill – 769 feet and 749 feet above sea level in Strichen and Rathen parishes, about six and a half miles south-south-west of Fraserburgh – made it a landmark for mariners, who were told to 'Keep Mormond Hill a handspike high and Rattray Briggs you'll not come nigh'. In 1870 W. F. Cordiner of Mormond House arranged for the outline of a stag to be etched on the hill's seaward side. Made of white quartzite stones found on the hill, covering nearly an acre and about 240 feet from antlers to hooves, the stag made the hill more conspicuous. Earlier in the nineteenth century, the white horse of Mormond was etched on the Strichen side of the hill, allegedly to commemorate a war horse used by Lord Lovat, a local laird. The outlines of the horse and the stag were camouflaged during the Second World War to prevent the Luftwaffe using them as landmarks.

The *Statistical Account* of 1792 says three cairns – on Memsie Moor in Rathen Parish, about four miles south-south-west of Fraserburgh – were 'thought to be monuments of the burials of some eminent men'. It suggests the cairns 'contained the graves of some chiefs who fell there' in battle against Danish raiders. The *New Statistical Account* of 1840 reports that the mound shown here, fifteen feet high and 60 feet in circumference at the base, was the sole survivor of the three cairns. When dismantled, one cairn revealed a partially vitrified base. A short iron-handled sword, several human skulls, and an urn 'of peculiar shape, containing calcined bones' were found in the other.

Rathen Station.

Around 45 miles northwards from Aberdeen and between two and three miles southward from the terminus at Fraserburgh, Rathen was the last public station on the Formartine and Buchan Railway. Lord Saltoun was recompensed for facilitating the completion of the last section of the line when Philorth Station, over a mile north of Rathen, was designated 'private for Philorth House'. From 1926 the timetable included Philorth among the public stations.

In 1870 St Ethernan's Kirk was replaced by this Gothic building, Rathen Parish Church (now Rathen West). Rathen is said to mean fort on the river. South-eastward from the church, Trefor Hill, which was formerly 'fortified' by walls of stone and earth, supports this derivation. However, Rathen may commemorate St Ethernan, an evangelist who dwelt in his hermitage (St Eddren's Slack) on Mormond Hill, where he died in 668 'amid the rigours of winter cold'. John and Ann Greig of Mosstown of Cairnbulg, ancestors of the Norwegian composer Edvard Grieg (note the different spelling) are buried in the old St Ethernan's Kirk graveyard. Edvard's great grandfather, a consul in Bergen, crossed and re-crossed the North Sea twice yearly to take communion in St Ethernan's!